W9-BVU-364

Abraham Lincoln

Civil War President

Colonial Leaders

Lord Baltimore
English Politician and Colonist

Benjamin Banneker
American Mathematician and Astronomer

Sir William Berkeley
Governor of Virginia

William Bradford
Governor of Plymouth Colony

Jonathan Edwards
Colonial Religious Leader

Benjamin Franklin
American Statesman, Scientist, and Writer

Anne Hutchinson
Religious Leader

Cotton Mather
Author, Clergyman, and Scholar

Increase Mather
Clergyman and Scholar

James Oglethorpe
Humanitarian and Soldier

William Penn
Founder of Democracy

Sir Walter Raleigh
English Explorer and Author

Caesar Rodney
American Patriot

John Smith
English Explorer and Colonist

Miles Standish
Plymouth Colony Leader

Peter Stuyvesant
Dutch Military Leader

George Whitefield
Clergyman and Scholar

Roger Williams
Founder of Rhode Island

John Winthrop
Politician and Statesman

John Peter Zenger
Free Press Advocate

Revolutionary War Leaders

John Adams
Second U.S. President

Ethan Allen
Revolutionary Hero

Benedict Arnold
Traitor to the Cause

King George III
English Monarch

Nathanael Greene
Military Leader

Nathan Hale
Revolutionary Hero

Alexander Hamilton
First U.S. Secretary of the Treasury

John Hancock
President of the Continental Congress

Patrick Henry
American Statesman and Speaker

John Jay
First Chief Justice of the Supreme Court

Thomas Jefferson
Author of the Declaration of Independence

John Paul Jones
Father of the U.S. Navy

Lafayette
French Freedom Fighter

James Madison
Father of the Constitution

Francis Marion
The Swamp Fox

James Monroe
American Statesman

Thomas Paine
Political Writer

Paul Revere
American Patriot

Betsy Ross
American Patriot

George Washington
First U.S. President

Famous Figures of the Civil War Era

Jefferson Davis
Confederate President

Frederick Douglass
Abolitionist and Author

Ulysses S. Grant
Military Leader and President

Stonewall Jackson
Confederate General

Robert E. Lee
Confederate General

Abraham Lincoln
Civil War President

William Sherman
Union General

Harriet Beecher Stowe
Author of Uncle Tom's Cabin

Sojourner Truth
Abolitionist, Suffragist, and Preacher

Harriet Tubman
Leader of the Underground Railroad

Abraham Lincoln

Civil War President

John F. Grabowski

Arthur M. Schlesinger, jr.
Senior Consulting Editor

Chelsea House Publishers

Philadelphia

Produced by 21st Century Publishing and Communications, Inc.
New York, NY. http://www.21cpc.com

CHELSEA HOUSE PUBLISHERS
Production Manager Pamela Loos
Art Director Sara Davis
Director of Photography Judy L. Hasday
Managing Editor James D. Gallagher
Senior Production Editor J. Christopher Higgins

Staff for *ABRAHAM LINCOLN*
Project Editor Anne Hill
Associate Art Director Takeshi Takahashi
Series Design Keith Trego

The Chelsea House World Wide Web address is
http://www.chelseahouse.com

First Printing
1 3 5 7 9 8 6 4 2

Library of Congress Cataloging-in-Publication Data

Grabowski, John F.
    Abraham Lincoln / John F. Grabowski.
      p.   cm. — (Famous figures of the Civil War era)
    Includes bibliographical references (p.).
    ISBN 0-7910-6004-7
      1. Lincoln, Abraham, 1809–1865—Juvenile literature. 2. Presidents
—United States—Biography—Juvenile literature. [1. Lincoln, Abraham,
1809–1865. 2. Presidents.] I. Title. II. Series.

E457.905 .G69   2000
973.7'092—dc21
[B]

00-038399
CIP

Publisher's Note: In Colonial, Revolutionary War, and Civil War Era
America, there were no standard rules for spelling, punctuation,
capitalization, or grammar. Some of the quotations that appear in
the Colonial Leaders, Revolutionary War Leaders, and Famous
Figures of the Civil War Era series come from original documents
and letters written during this time in history. Original quotations
reflect writing inconsistencies of the period.

Contents

Abraham Lincoln was born in this log cabin in Kentucky. Even though he grew up in the country and had little formal schooling, Abe later became a lawyer, a congressman, and president of the United States.

From a Log Cabin in Kentucky

The weather was chilly at Sinking Spring farm near Hodgenville, Kentucky. It was the morning of February 12, 1809. Ten-year-old Dennis Hanks was hard at work doing his chores. Suddenly, Thomas Lincoln ran out of the forest in Denny's direction. Tom's wife, Nancy, was Denny's cousin.

"Nancy's got a baby boy," yelled Tom.

Tom and Denny raced back to the family's log cabin. There lay Nancy with the baby in her arms. Nancy's two-year-old daughter, Sarah, sat next to her.

"What you goin' to name him, Nancy?" asked Denny.

"Abraham," replied the mother of the new-born. It was the name of Tom's father. Grand-father Lincoln had been killed by Indians in 1786. He had crossed the Allegheny Mountains with Daniel Boone some years before.

Tom grew up with no formal schooling. He had never learned to read or write. In 1806, he married Nancy Hanks. He supported his family as a farmer and carpenter. They had three children. Sarah was Abe's older sister. A younger brother named Thomas died soon after birth.

When Abe was three years old, his family moved to a farm in Knob Creek, Kentucky. Here he ran and played in the green hills. One time, the boy fell in a nearby creek. Luckily, he was pulled out before he drowned.

Abe's father was a very hard worker. It was difficult for him to make his farm a success. Kentucky was a slave state. Tom was a Baptist

When Abe was young he had to do chores, like the boys shown here. By the time he was a teenager he was strong, good with an ax, and able to help his father clear land in the wilderness of Indiana.

who did not believe in **slavery**. He believed that all men should be treated equally.

Records of land ownership in Kentucky were not well kept. Other men claimed Tom's land. Tom was in danger of losing it. In 1816, he decided to move his family to Indiana. Indiana had just entered the Union as the 19th state. Slavery was forbidden there. Tom saw this as a chance to start a new life for his family.

The family traveled to the southwest corner of Indiana. There, Tom cleared land for a cabin in a community called Pigeon Creek. Abe was growing up to be a tall, strong young boy. He was handy with an ax. He helped his father by clearing the underbrush.

Life in the family's new home was very difficult. The uncleared **wilderness** presented new dangers. "It was a wild region," Abe would recall, "with many bears and other wild animals still in the woods."

Tom Lincoln and his family arrived in Indiana in December of 1816. The weather was cold. There was no time to build a cabin before the first big snow fell. Instead, Tom built a "half-faced camp." This was a kind of temporary shelter. Three sides were formed from logs. On the fourth side was a roaring fire. This served two purposes. First, it provided the family with warmth; second, it kept away wild animals, such as grizzly bears and wolves. When warmer weather arrived in the spring, Tom built a new cabin.

In 1818, Abe's mother died of milk sickness. She was only 34 years old. Milk sickness was caused by drinking infected milk from cows who ate the poisonous white snakeroot plant. Tom, Abe, and Sarah missed Nancy very much. They buried her on a hill near the cabin.

Twelve-year-old Sarah tried her best to help with the housekeeping chores. It was extremely difficult. Tom soon realized he needed someone to help take care of the house.

The next spring, Abe's father traveled back to Kentucky to look for a new wife. There he met a widow named Sarah Bush Johnston. Tom had known Sarah before he married Nancy Hanks. Sarah had three children of her own. Tom soon married Sarah and returned to Indiana. Abe loved his stepmother. She was a kind and loving person who treated him like her own son. "Abe was a good boy," said Sarah, "[who] never gave me a cross word or look. . . . He was kind to everybody and to everything."

Abe was a thoughtful boy who always

helped others. He had a strong desire to learn and was always asking questions. Unfortunately, he had very little formal education. He attended "blab" schools for a total of about one year. In these schools, pupils studied out loud. Abe learned how to read and write and do basic arithmetic. He continued his education at home by reading everything he could find. "It didn't seem natural to see a feller read like that," recalled Dennis Hanks. Abe carried a book with him at all times. In this way, he could read whenever he took a break from his chores around the farm. His favorite books included *The Adventures of Robinson Crusoe, The Arabian Nights,* and the Bible. He was especially fond of Parson Mason Weems's *Life of Washington.* This was a biography of the nation's first president.

Abe grew into an impressive young man. He stood nearly 6' 4" tall and was very strong. He had black hair and deep-set eyes. He had high cheekbones, large ears, and thick eyebrows. Everyone who met him could not help but remember him.

Abe was a big help around the homestead. By now he had become an expert at using an ax. "If you heard him fellin' trees in a clearin'," said Denny Hanks, "you would say that there was three men at work by the way the trees fell." Abe often split logs into fence rails for their neighbors. He also dug wells, chopped down trees, and did other odd jobs. In this way, he earned money to help his family.

When Abe was 19, his sister Sarah died during childbirth. Since he was very close to his sister, he was deeply saddened by her death. Shortly after, his fortunes took a turn for the better. He was offered a job on a flatboat by a local merchant named James Gentry. Together with Gentry's son Allen, Abe helped guide the boatload of farm produce down the Ohio and Mississippi Rivers to New Orleans. Young Abe was shocked at the size of the city. Here he came into contact with slaves for the first time in his life. Abe was angered by the thought of

This early view of New Orleans shows ships on the Mississippi River. Abe's riverboat trip to New Orleans as a teenager was important because there he saw slaves for the first time. He realized then he would always oppose slavery.

slavery. He never forgot the sight of black men, women, and children being sold like cattle.

When Abe returned home, his father decided to move once again. The family traveled 200 miles by wagon to Illinois. They settled on uncleared land along the Sangamon River. Tom, Abe, and Abe's stepbrother helped build a log cabin for the family. The next year, a shop-keeper named Denton Offutt hired Abe for another trip to New Orleans. First, though, Abe and two other men had to build a flatboat. Offutt paid them each $12 a month to do the work. When they finished, they floated their cargo down to New Orleans.

When he returned home this time, Abe faced a big decision. He was now 22 years old. What did he want to do with his life? He knew one thing for certain. He did not want to spend his life doing hard labor like his father. A life on the **frontier** was not for him. He had developed an interest in the law. Perhaps he could become a lawyer and use his mind to help others.

Over the years, Abe had grown apart from his father. He decided to leave his family and set out on his own. He moved to New Salem, Illinois. His friend, Offutt, was going to open a general store there. Offutt offered Abe a job, and he accepted. He was ready to make his mark on the world.

This photograph shows Abe Lincoln as a young man. His early years in an Illinois debating society were good preparation both for his law business and his political career.

Political Leader

New Salem was a growing community of about 100 people. The Sangamon River flowed nearby. While in New Salem, Abe continued educating himself. He joined the New Salem Debating Society. This gave him experience speaking in front of groups of people. It also taught him how to express his ideas clearly. "He was a fine speaker," recalled one debater.

Abe made many friends in the community. One was a rowdy young man named Jack Armstrong. Armstrong was the leader of a gang of young toughs known as the Clary's Grove Boys. He was also the best wrestler in New Salem. One day, he challenged Abe to a wrestling match. Abe stood up to the roughneck and accepted. With Armstrong's gang watching, the two young men began their battle. When the fight began to turn in Abe's favor, Armstrong's thugs joined the brawl. Abe released Armstrong. He then offered to fight all the others, one at a time. Impressed by his opponent's courage and fighting ability, Armstrong stopped his gang. He offered Abe his hand in friendship. The two men became close friends.

Abe learned a lot about local and national affairs by reading newspapers. He became interested in finding ways to help others. He was in favor of local improvements, such as better roads and more schools. As Abe once said, "I view [education] as the most important subject which we as a people may be engaged in." In March of 1832, Abe decided to run for the state **legislature**. He ran as a member of the Whig Party. The Whigs favored a strong central government.

Abe's **campaign** was interrupted by war with

Chief Black Hawk (left) and his son led the Sac Indians in a war against the U.S. government. Abe signed up to fight the Indians, but he never saw action and soon returned home to work on his political campaign.

the Indians. Chief Black Hawk led a group of Sac Indians into northern Illinois. They were trying to take back lands the government had taken away from them. Volunteers, including Abe, offered their services. Abe was voted captain of his small company of men. But the Indians were defeated before he saw any action. Abe later joked about his experiences. He told friends how he survived "a good many bloody battles with mosquitoes." Abe returned to New Salem two weeks before the election.

Abe made many speeches, but time was running short. He lost the election, finishing 8th out of 13 **candidates**. In New Salem, though, he won nearly every vote. He was very popular with those people who knew him. He impressed them with his intelligence, honesty, and sense of humor.

After the election, Abe took on several jobs. A local businessman named William F. Berry needed help with his general store. Abe became his partner. Unfortunately, the store failed. Abe was left with a debt of more than $1,000. Even though it was difficult, he eventually repaid all the money.

Then Abe was appointed village postmaster of New Salem. He also worked as an assistant **surveyor** for the county. In this job, he helped lay out the boundaries for farms, roads, and new towns. These two jobs gave him an income. They also helped him to meet more people who were also potential voters.

Abe never lost his interest in politics. He decided to run for the legislature again in 1834, when he was 25. Lincoln wanted the country to develop a better system of transportation. In this way, he believed the nation would expand and become stronger. "The poorest and most thinly populated [areas] would be greatly benefited by the opening of good roads, and in the clearing of navigable streams," he said. "There cannot justly be any objection to having railroads and canals."

When all the votes had been counted, Abe finished second out of the 13 candidates. The top four finishers were elected. Abe was on his way to the state capital of Vandalia as a member of the state legislature.

Abe wanted to do the best job he could. He realized it was important for him to know as much as possible about the law. John Todd Stuart, a candidate from another district, urged him to continue his studies. Abe decided to become a lawyer. In Abe's day, most lawyers did not go to college. They studied law on their own until they could pass the **bar** examination. Stuart loaned him many law books. Abe passed the exam in 1836 and became a practicing attorney.

Abe was reelected in 1836, 1838, and 1840. As he gained experience, he also gained supporters. His reputation grew quickly. During his second term in office, Abe had to face an issue that was threatening to divide the country in two. It was the matter of slavery.

Slavery had been introduced to the colonies in 1619. Blacks were brought over on Dutch warships from Africa to Jamestown, Virginia. They were sold as slaves to wealthy farmers and **plantation** owners. Slavery quickly became established, especially in the South. Although many people opposed slavery, many others supported it.

Those who were against slavery were called **abolitionists**. Many abolitionists in the North demanded that all slaves be freed. Southerners

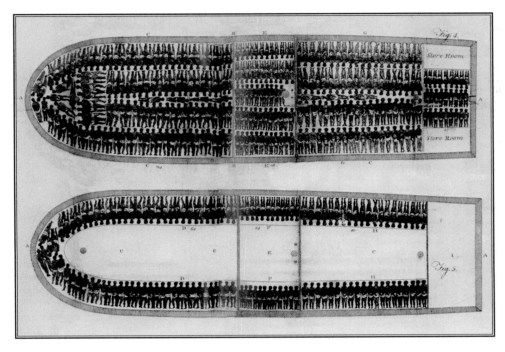

Slaves were first brought to the American colonies in crowded slave ships like these. Farmers and plantation owners in the South needed slaves to work their land, while many Northerners wanted all slaves to be freed.

claimed they needed slaves to work their farms.

Illinois was not a slave state. But many people there did not want slaves to have equal rights. Abe was strongly against slavery. He felt it was wrong. "Whenever I hear anyone arguing for slavery," he once said, "I feel a strong impulse to see it tried on him personally." The young legislator feared that slavery would split the country.

Abe did not agree with the methods used by the abolitionists. Many wanted to use violence to end slavery. Abe did not think the federal government should interfere with slavery in states where it already existed. He thought it would eventually die out on its own. More importantly, he did not want it to spread to any new territories or states. The issue of slavery would trouble him the rest of his life.

In 1837, Abe's friend, John Todd Stuart, invited him to become his law partner. The Illinois state capital was about to be moved from Vandalia to Springfield. Stuart expected his business to expand. He needed someone to help him share the work. Abe gladly accepted the offer. He moved to Springfield that April. He lived in a room above a store owned by Joshua F. Speed. Over the years, Speed became one of Abe's closest friends.

Around this time, Abe met an attractive, intelligent young woman named Mary Ann Todd. Mary was the daughter of a wealthy banker. She lived in Springfield with her sister, Eli:

and Elizabeth's husband, Ninian W. Edv

Edwards's father had been governor of Illine

Mary and Abe began seeing each other r_gu-larly. They soon fell in love and decided to get married. The Edwardses objected, though. They felt a backwoodsman like Abe was not good enough for Mary. Abe began to doubt if he would be able to support a family. He decided to call the engagement off. The next few months were the worst of his life. "I am now the most miserable man living," wrote Abe. "To remain as I am is impossible; I must die or be better, it appears to me."

Mary and Abe's love did not die. After a year apart, they began to see each other again. Mary's family finally gave in. The young lawyer and the wealthy society woman were married in 1842. The following year, their first son was born. They named him Robert Todd. A second son, Edward Baker, was born two years later. William Wallace followed in 1850 and Thomas in 1853. Thomas was nicknamed Tad since he

This portrait of the Lincoln family includes Abe, Mary, and their sons Robert and Tad. Abe and Mary had a happy marriage and were devoted parents.

squirmed like a tadpole as a baby.

By this time, Abe had formed a new partnership with a lawyer named Stephen T. Logan. This partnership lasted until 1844, when Abe opened his own office. He took on a junior partner named William Herndon. Abe was on his way to becoming one of the top lawyers in the state of Illinois. His reputation for honesty helped him win many cases.

Although Abe was no longer a member of the state legislature, his interest in politics was as strong as

The Lincolns adored their children. In the eyes of their parents, the boys could do no wrong. Abe and Mary rarely disciplined the boys, even when their behavior was unruly. This bothered many of their friends. As Abe's law partner, William Herndon, once said, "I have felt many and many a time that I wanted to wring the necks of those little brats and pitch them out of the windows." Other friends felt the same way.

ever. He decided to run for Congress. Abe's reputation had spread far and wide. In 1846, he was nominated by the Whig Party to run for the U.S. House of Representatives. Abe defeated Democratic candidate Peter Cartwright to win the election. The next year, the new congressman and his family moved to the nation's capital in Washington, D.C.

When Abe went to Washington as a congressman, he worked in the House of Representatives, shown here. Abe worked hard, but after one term he went back to his law business in Illinois.

An Elected Representative of the People

When they first arrived in Washington, D.C., the Lincolns lived in a boarding-house across the street from the Capitol building. Mary did not like the city. After just three months, she moved back to Kentucky with their sons. Abe remained in Washington by himself.

In 1846 the United States went to war with Mexico. Some years earlier, American settlers had begun living in Texas. At the time, Texas was part of Mexico. In 1836, the settlers rebelled against the government. They declared themselves a new nation, called the Lone Star Republic. In 1845,

Texas joined the Union as the 28th state. Mexico refused to recognize the new state's borders. Fighting soon broke out. Eventually, the United States, under President James K. Polk, declared war against Mexico. After two years of fighting, Mexico surrendered to U.S. troops. As part of the treaty ending the war, the United States received a large parcel of land. It stretched all the way to the Pacific Ocean.

Many Americans disagreed with the Mexican War. Abe was one of them. He felt the United States had been the **aggressor**, rather than the Mexicans. He spoke out against President Polk in the House of Representatives. Abe believed Polk had started the war to capture Mexican territory. Abe's stand angered many Illinois voters. They felt he was taking the enemy's side. His reputation was badly damaged.

Before Abe accepted the nomination to Congress, he had agreed to serve only one term. In this way, other Whig candidates would have a chance to win the post. Abe thought he

In this drawing, American soldiers prepare for a battle during the war against Mexico. Abe disagreed with the war; his speeches on the subject angered the president and Congress because he seemed to be siding with America's enemy.

would be appointed commissioner of the General Land Office at the end of his term. But when his term was over, he was not offered the job because of the reaction to his position against Polk. So instead, he returned to his law office in Springfield. He was joined there by Mary and their sons. Abe was defeated, but not discouraged.

Abe's work was interrupted in late 1849. His son, Edward, fell seriously ill and died two months later. Abe and his wife were devastated. Mary cried for weeks. Abe became even more deeply involved in his law practice.

Abe did a great deal of traveling for his work. He tried cases in many faraway courthouses. He enjoyed this part of his job because it allowed him to meet new people from different regions. His reputation grew, and

In 1854, Abe defended Jack Armstrong's son, Duff, in a murder case. A witness said he clearly saw Duff Armstrong kill James Metzger during a fight. The man said he was sure of what he saw because the full moon was shining directly overhead.

Abe pulled an almanac out of his pocket. An almanac is a book that contains a calendar. It also gives information about the weather for the year. According to the almanac, the moon was low in the sky on the night of the murder, and not shining brightly overhead. Armstrong was found not guilty of the charges.

he became one of the most respected lawyers in all of Illinois.

The end of the Mexican War had brought up the issue of slavery once again. Would the new territories acquired from Mexico enter the Union as slave or free states?

Many farmers in the slave states needed the free labor to take care of their crops, especially cotton. Cotton was not a very profitable crop. It required too much time to separate the cotton fibers from the seeds by hand. But in 1793 Eli Whitney had invented the cotton gin. This machine performed the job much faster. The demand for cotton increased. More workers were needed to plant the cotton and to pick it. This caused an increase in the demand for slaves. The crop came to be known as "king cotton."

Some cotton farmers wanted to expand to the West. Northerners did not want slavery in these new territories. The Missouri **Compromise** of 1820 banned slavery in the territories of Kansas and Nebraska. In 1854, Congress passed the

Kansas-Nebraska Act. This act was introduced by Illinois Senator Stephen Douglas. It said that these territories should be allowed to decide the slavery issue for themselves.

Abe was shocked. If slavery were allowed to expand, it would be harder to put an end to it. He felt that slavery hurt whites as well as blacks. Whites would be forced to compete with slaves for jobs. Abe had always believed in the words of the Declaration of Independence. He felt that both blacks and whites should be entitled to the rights it described.

As settlers moved into Kansas, violence broke out between the rival sides. The region became known as "Bleeding Kansas." Soon after, the Supreme Court reached a decision in the case of Dred Scott. Scott was a slave who had been brought by his master to free territory. When they returned to Missouri, Scott sued for his freedom. He argued that he should be free since he had spent time in free territory. The justices disagreed with him. They ruled that a slave was a piece of

As more and more cotton was grown in the South, more slaves were needed to work in the cotton fields (shown here). The issue of the expansion of slavery was one of the main reasons Abe Lincoln returned to politics.

property owned by a master. Therefore slaves had no rights under the law. They could be taken anywhere, just like a suitcase. Chief Justice Roger Taney further ruled that the Constitution gave states the right to own slaves. That meant that the Missouri Compromise was unconstitutional.

The Kansas-Nebraska Act had stirred up Abe's emotions. He decided to return to politics. Many Whigs, like Abe, had become upset with their party. They formed the Republican Party in response. Republicans were opposed to slavery because they felt it would not be good for whites. They did not want to do away with slavery in the South. They simply did not want it to be allowed to spread to the West. Even though Abe hated slavery, he accepted it as the law of the nation.

In 1858, the Republicans nominated Abe to run against Stephen Douglas for a seat in the Senate. While campaigning in Springfield, Abe cautioned that slavery could destroy the nation. "A house divided against itself cannot stand," warned Abe. "I believe this government cannot endure, permanently half slave and half free."

Abe suggested that the two men meet in a series of debates in the fall of 1858. Douglas agreed. The seven debates captured the nation's attention. Large crowds came to hear them speak. Douglas, known as "The Little Giant," argued that each state should have the right to decide if it wanted to be slave or free. Abe, called "Long Abe" or "Honest Abe," wanted slavery confined to the South. In this way, he hoped it would eventually die out.

The final vote in the election was very close. At that time, elections were not decided by direct popular vote. The state legislatures decided who would go to the Senate. The Republicans did not win enough seats to place Abe. Douglas was declared the winner.

Although he lost the election, Abe was not discouraged. "The fight must go on," he told a friend. "The cause of civil liberty must not be surrendered at the end of one or even one hundred defeats." Because of the debates, Abe became nationally known. His intelligence and political skills won him many supporters. Abe began thinking about his political future.

By 1860, Abe was being mentioned as a possible candidate for president. But he had some doubts about being the right person for

As the Republican nominee for president, Abe Lincoln (left) defeated Democratic candidates John C. Breckenridge (center) and Stephen A. Douglas in the 1860 election. Abe won a majority in every Northern state.

the job. In a letter to *Rock Island Register* editor Thomas J. Pickett, Abe wrote, "I must . . . say I do not think myself fit for the presidency." Other Illinois Republicans did not have such doubts. They chose Abe as their candidate at the state convention in May. The following week, he was nominated as the Republican candidate at the national convention in Chicago. Hannibal Hamlin of Maine was nominated for vice president.

On November 6, 1860, Abraham Lincoln was elected as the 16th president of the United States of America, succeeding James Buchanan. He defeated Northern Democrat Stephen Douglas, Southern Democrat John C. Breckinridge, and Constitutional Union Party candidate John Bell. Abe carried every Northern state.

Southern leaders were upset with the results of the election. Some states were already threatening to **secede**, or leave, the Union. They wanted to form their own slave nation. On December 20, South Carolina became the first state to do so. Abe's worst fears were being realized. He had not even been **inaugurated** yet and the nation was beginning to split apart.

Abe entertained the crowd as he raised the flag at Philadelphia's Independence Hall on his way to Washington for his inauguration in 1861. A local newspaper reported that "for a full three minutes the cheers continued."

The War Between the North and the South

1nauguration Day was March 4, 1861. By then, six other states—Mississippi, Florida, Alabama, Georgia, Louisiana, and Texas—had followed South Carolina and seceded from the Union. Four more states—Virginia, Arkansas, North Carolina, and Tennessee—were about to do so. In February, the states that seceded from the Union met in Montgomery, Alabama, to form the Confederate States of America. They selected Mississippi native Jefferson Davis as their first president. Davis had been a senator from Mississippi and secretary of war under President Franklin Pierce. Alexander

H. Stephens of Georgia was selected as vice president. "Our new government," said Stephens, "is founded . . . upon the great truth that the Negro is not equal to the white man; that slavery . . . is his natural and moral condition."

Davis was inaugurated on February 18. He had not really wanted the office, but he accepted it because his fellow Southerners wanted him to do so. Davis strongly believed in the Southern way of life and slavery was a very important part of it.

All attempts to bring the states back together completely failed. The Southerners would not back down from their demands. They wanted

Most pictures of Abe show him with a beard. He did not have one until 1860. Shortly before the election, he received a letter from a young girl named Grace Bedell. In her letter, Grace suggested that the clean-shaven Abe grow a beard. "All the ladies like whiskers," she wrote, "and they would tease their husbands to vote for you." Abe took her advice. He began to grow a beard. In March, he took office as the first bearded president of the United States.

slavery to be allowed to spread to other territories. With no compromise possible, the Confederacy prepared for war.

Rumors were already spreading about attempts on the new president's life. The army was put on alert. Some people thought that Southerners would try to take control of the capital. Soldiers watched from rooftops as Abe was sworn in. Fortunately, the inauguration went off without any problems.

Shortly after Abe became president, the country faced a major crisis. Fort Sumter was a U.S. army outpost in Charleston Harbor, off the coast of South Carolina. The governor of that state wanted control of the fort. Charleston was an important international port. If the Confederacy did not control the harbor, it would be difficult to establish itself as a new nation. So the Southerners decided to take over Fort Sumter in order to control the harbor.

The fort was running low on supplies. It

No one was killed in the attack on Fort Sumter that marked the start of the Civil War. But one person did die just after the battle. During the surrender ceremony, a 50-gun salute was delivered. As the guns were being reloaded for the last time, a spark touched off an early explosion. Daniel Hough, a Union private, was killed in the blast. Hot ashes from the explosion fell on the ammunition that was stacked below. Some of these shells exploded, injuring five other men.

could not hold out against the Southerners for long. If the Union abandoned the fort it would be seen as a sign of weakness. To do otherwise might bring on a war. After much thought, Abe decided to send supply ships to the fort. He would not allow the federal government to be bullied by threats. When the Union supply ships approached the city, the rebels opened fire on the fort. It was 4:30 A.M. on April 12, 1861. The Civil War had begun. It would be the bloodiest war in the history of the nation.

Union Major Robert Anderson surrendered the fort to General Pierre Beauregard of the Confederate army a week later. The next day, Abe called for 75,000 volunteers to put

The Confederate army used 4,000 shells in the first 36 hours of its attack on Fort Sumter, South Carolina (shown here). After this first battle of the Civil War, both the North and the South gathered their armies, but both sides believed the war would be over quickly.

down the Southern rebellion. A strong wave of patriotism swept through the North. Both the North and the South prepared troops for the coming war.

Most Northerners felt the fighting would end quickly. The South controlled 11 states while the North had 23. This gave the North a tremendous population advantage. In addition, the North was the more industrialized region. The South's economy was mainly based on farming. The one advantage the South had was in military intelligence. More skilled commanders came from the South, including the brilliant general Robert E. Lee. General Winfield Scott was commander of the Union forces. Abe had originally asked Lee to take command of the Union armies. Lee turned him down and decided to remain on the side of his native Virginia.

The federal government was in a vulnerable position. The nation's capital lay just across the Potomac River from Virginia. On July 21, Union forces under the command of General Irvin McDowell crossed the river. They moved into Virginia, ready for combat. There they met Beauregard's Southern troops near a small stream known as Bull Run. Dozens of spectators watched the fighting, including politicians and their families. Many camped on hillsides with picnic baskets, waiting for the action to begin. They believed the Union forces would easily defeat the Southern troops.

The Southerners rallied behind a company of Virginians commanded by General Thomas J. Jackson. After several hours of fighting, the Union forces broke down and retreated to Washington. Jackson's resistance earned him the nickname "Stonewall." The South had won the first major land battle of the war.

Abe realized that he needed stronger military leaders. He named George B. McClellan general in chief of all the armies on November 1. McClellan replaced Scott, who was not well. McClellan strengthened Washington's defenses. He built up the army, eventually planning to attack Richmond, Virginia. The capital of the Confederacy had been moved to Richmond from Montgomery in May.

McClellan did not march south, though. He said he needed more time, more men, and more supplies.

By early 1862, the war took up all of Abe's waking moments. In February, another great tragedy added to his sadness. His 11-year-old son, Willie, fell ill with a fever. Willie's condition worsened, and he died on February 20. Abe and his wife were crushed. Mary never completely recovered from losing a second young son to illness.

During this time, the pace of the war was increasing. Abe decided to take a more active role in controlling the day-to-day conduct of the war. He used his presidential powers to enforce several unpopular policies. He suspended the right of **habeas corpus**, which protects citizens from arrest without being told the reasons. Thousands of people were jailed as traitors this way, without going to trial. Abe felt these measures were necessary to preserve the Union. His opponents thought he was

**General Ulysses S. Grant (front row, without a hat)
leads his generals in battle. After several Civil War
victories, Grant became a war hero in the North.
He later became president of the United States.**

abusing his powers.

Early in 1862, the Union began having
some success in the West. General Ulysses S.

Grant led the troops to several victories. In doing so, he became a national hero. When Grant defeated the Southern troops at Fort Donelson in Tennessee, he demanded, "No terms but immediate and unconditional surrender." From that time on, people said his initials—U.S.G—stood for "Unconditional Surrender" Grant.

At Shiloh, in southwestern Tennessee, Grant's forces were attacked by Confederate troops led by General Albert Sidney Johnston. About 77,000 soldiers took part in the battle. Most of them were inexperienced recruits. Many did not even know how to handle their rifles. More than 23,000 were either killed or injured in the fighting. Grant's men held their position. It was the largest battle in the nation's history. Many people wanted Grant replaced after the stand-off. Abe refused to listen to them. "I can't spare this man," he said. "He fights."

In the East, the Union was still having

problems. In late June, McClellan was finally ready to advance into Richmond. He had been waiting for additional troops to meet him. But rumors of a possible assault on Washington caused the troops to be recalled to the capital. McClellan's strategy failed. His troops were held off by forces under the command of Robert E. Lee. Lee had just been appointed commander in chief of the Army of Northern Virginia on June 1.

Abe was beginning to lose confidence in McClellan's command. Many lives were being lost. There was no end to the war in sight. Abe decided to replace McClellan with General Henry W. Halleck. But Halleck proved to be no better. Most important decisions continued to rest on Abe's shoulders. He realized adjustments were in order. "We must change our tactics or lose the war," he decided.

As the conflict dragged on, the slavery issue became even more complicated. Originally, Abe was willing to leave slavery in the

This painting, showing Abe with a former slave, Sojourner Truth, commemorates his signing of the Emancipation Proclamation, which changed the course of the Civil War.

South if this would restore the Union. After the South was beaten, slavery would die out on its own. As he stated, "We didn't go into the war to put down slavery, but to put the flag back."

Abolitionists, on the other hand, wanted all slaves freed immediately. Abe was afraid to do that. He thought that might cause the slave states that bordered on the South–Kentucky, Missouri, Maryland, and Delaware–to leave the Union. He suggested that slaves in the border states be freed gradually. Slave owners would be given money from the government as payment. This offer was turned down by the states.

It soon became obvious to Abe that slavery had to be abolished. Doing so would lead to a quicker end to the war. The freed slaves would be willing to enlist in the Union army, which would weaken the South. This raised another question. Did the president have the power to abolish slavery in states where it was legal? His advisors believed he did, because it was wartime.

By July 22, 1862, Abe had made a very

important decision. He told his advisors of his plan. He would issue a statement freeing the slaves in all states that did not return to the Union by January 1, 1863. This, he said, was "a military necessity, absolutely essential to the preservation of the Union."

A month later, he repeated this main goal to Horace Greeley, the editor of the *New York Tribune.* The president said, "If I could save the Union without freeing any slaves I would do it; if I could save it by freeing all the slaves, I would do it, and if I could do it by freeing some and leaving others alone, I would do that."

Abe planned to make the announcement as soon as the Union won an important victory in the East. In mid-September, McClellan's Union troops repelled the Confederate army in a bloody battle at Antietam Creek in Maryland. But he did not follow Lee, and the remaining rebel forces escaped back to Virginia. Both sides suffered serious casualties, but the battle was considered a win for the Union.

The following week, Abe issued his proclamation to the newspapers. On New Year's Day, Abe signed the historic paper. Slaves in the Confederate states officially became free. The Emancipation Proclamation changed the entire character of the war. "If my name ever goes into history," said Abe, "it will be for this act."

Abe Lincoln (right) confers with General Grant (center) and General Sherman aboard the Union steamer *River Queen* in March 1865. The primary topic of their discussion was the terms of the upcoming peace.

Victory and Tragedy

The Emancipation Proclamation did not actually free any slaves. It only applied to slaves in the Confederate states—so it could not be enforced. But as these territories were taken back by the Union, slaves gained their freedom.

The Emancipation Proclamation aroused different emotions in different people. Many Northerners were glad that the slaves had been freed. Others were upset. They had wanted the Union to be saved, but did not want blacks to have the same rights as they did. They did not want blacks in the Union army. They did not like the idea of blacks being allowed to carry guns. Still others just wanted the war over and the troops home. They did not care if slavery was outlawed. Riots broke out in cities where people were against the draft. Hundreds of people died.

Through everything, Abe remained strong. He refused to change his plan to save the Union. In March, he signed the Conscription Act. This law gave the War Department the power to draft men between the ages of 20 and 46 for military service. This service could be avoided by paying a fee of $300. In this way, many rich people got away without being drafted. The poorer classes did not find the act fair. This led to rioting in many cities. In New York, nearly 1,000 people died in a week of protests in July.

The Northern armies continued to struggle. Abe was still searching for a strong military leader. Troops under generals Ambrose E. Burnside and Joseph "Fighting Joe" Hooker both suffered decisive defeats in Virginia. Burnside lost at Fredericksburg, Virginia, and Hooker at Chancellorsville in the same state. Things did not look good for the Union. Rebel troops under General Robert E. Lee fought bravely. But the South did suffer an important loss. General "Stonewall" Jackson was killed in the battle at Chancellorsville. Jackson was Lee's best general.

Lee decided that the time was right for another assault on the North. Perhaps a major city like Baltimore could be eventually be captured. As Lee continued moving north, Abe put General George G. Meade in charge of Union forces. On July 1, 1863, the two sides met on the battlefields of Gettysburg, Pennsylvania. It was the turning point of the entire war.

July 3 was the worst day of fighting. Fourteen thousand men under Southern general George Pickett advanced against the Union troops. Northern soldiers shot down the rebels as they tried to cross nearly a mile of open fields. Nearly 10,000 men were killed or injured in the assault. It came to be known as Pickett's Charge.

Lee blamed himself for the loss. As the

remaining men returned to the Confederate lines, he sat upon his horse, Traveller. "It's all my fault," he was heard to say, "it's all my fault." On July 4, after three days of fighting, Lee's army began its retreat to Virginia. But Meade did not follow. The Southern troops managed to escape once again.

Lee's Army of Northern Virginia was composed of 75,000 men. The Army of the Potomac, under Meade, consisted of 88,000. The Battle of Gettysburg resulted in more than 50,000 casualties. More men fought and died at Gettysburg than at any single battle ever on American soil. Bodies of the dead and wounded covered the battlefield for days. It was decided that a national cemetery would be dedicated there for the fallen soldiers of both sides.

The dedication was set for November 19, 1863. The main speaker that afternoon was the former governor of Massachusetts, Edward Everett. When he had finished his two-hour speech, Abe stepped up to the platform. He gave a short two-minute speech. It has gone down as possibly the most famous in American history. In his Gettysburg Address, Abe stated his beliefs about the war. It was being fought, he said, to preserve the nation that had been created in 1776. The government was based on certain ideas and principles. A main one was that all men had the right to freedom. The war was a test to see if that kind of government could survive. "These dead shall not have died in vain," concluded the president, "that this nation, under God, shall have a new birth of freedom, and that government of the people, by the people, for the people, shall not perish from the earth."

In the meantime, Union forces had been making progress on the Western front. Troops led by Ulysses S. Grant won significant victories, including an important one at Vicksburg, Mississippi. The victory gave the North complete control of the Mississippi River. It had the effect of splitting the Confederacy in two.

Abe was becoming more impressed with Grant's leadership. In March of 1864, he made Grant general in chief of all Union armies.

Together, the two men worked on a plan to bring an end to the conflict. The "Grand Plan" called for putting pressure on the two major Confederate armies. If necessary, the Union army would attack them throughout the entire summer.

It was decided that Grant would lead his troops to Virginia. He would try to push Lee and the Army of Northern Virginia back toward the Southern capital of Richmond. Farther west, forces led by General William Tecumseh Sherman would attack General Joseph Johnston's Army of Tennessee. Sherman's troops would then move toward the Confederate city of Atlanta, Georgia. In this way, the Union would strike at the heart of the Confederacy.

In May 1864, the Union launched its two assaults. Grant attacked Lee's forces in an area of Virginia called the Wilderness. Despite days of fierce fighting, Grant could not defeat the Rebels. Lee's forces bravely resisted and held their ground. More than 50,000 Union soldiers were killed or wounded. Sherman's forces, likewise,

The Battle of Gettysburg, Pennsylvania, (shown here) was the turning point of the Civil War and the bloodiest battle ever fought on American soil.

could not break through in Georgia.

More and more Northerners were disappointed with the results of these battles. The death toll rose higher and higher with each passing day. The presidential election was scheduled for late that year. Many people hoped to see Abe replaced by someone who would end the fighting.

Abe's supporters eventually won out. He was nominated for a second term of office at the Republican National Convention in June. His Democratic opponent was none other than General George McClellan, former commander of the Union forces. McClellan promised to end the fighting. He said he would restore the Union and allow slavery to continue in the South. Abe began to fear that he might lose the election. "It seems exceedingly probable," he wrote, "that this Administration will not be re-elected."

The war continued to drag on. In July, the Union received another scare. Confederate forces under the command of General Jubal Early crossed the Potomac River into Maryland. They moved forward until they reached the borders of the capital. Rebel bullets flew over Abe's head as he watched the fighting in the distance. Early's troops were finally fought off by two divisions sent by Grant. The Union had successfully defended itself against the threat.

With election day getting nearer, good news came from General Sherman. His troops had stormed the city of Atlanta. The Southern stronghold had been destroyed and the city evacuated. And at Mobile Bay, off the Alabama coast, a fleet led by Union Admiral David G. Farragut successfully attacked Confederate ships guarding the important port of Mobile. It was the greatest naval battle of the war. The harbor had been mined with explosives. A Union ship was destroyed by one of these torpedoes. When the others stopped advancing, Farragut gave his famous order: "Full speed ahead."

Farragut's triumph was followed up by another important victory. General Philip Sheridan's troops defeated Early's forces in the Shenandoah Valley of Virginia. It appeared that the North was going to be victorious at last. With the end of the war in sight, Abe was reelected by a large margin.

Andrew Johnson of Tennessee was elected as vice president. Abe's policies and strategies had proved to be successful.

But Abe realized that his Emancipation Proclamation was not law. It could be overturned at any time by Congress or a future president. He wanted a constitutional amendment passed that would outlaw slavery. Congress agreed with the president. The Thirteenth Amendment to the Constitution was proposed. When passed, it would ban slavery in the United States of America.

A little more than a month later, Abe took the oath of office for his second term as president. In his Inaugural Address, he called for cooperation between the North and South. He did not want to punish the states that had left the Union. He wanted to help bring all the states together again.

Meanwhile, Union forces were advancing northward. Richmond was still under Confederate control, but Lee could not hold out much longer. On April 2, Grant's forces broke through Lee's defenses. Richmond was evacuated. Jefferson

Davis left the executive mansion and fled to Danville, Virginia. As they left Richmond, the Southerners burned down warehouses and bridges behind them. The city was left in ruins.

The remaining fighting ended soon afterward. On April 9, Robert E. Lee and Ulysses S. Grant met at Appomattox Court House in Virginia. There, Lee formally surrendered. Nine days later, Johnston surrendered to Sherman near Durham, North Carolina. Jefferson Davis was captured the following month and the war finally came to an end. It had lasted four years. About 650,000 people had lost their lives. However, the nation had survived, and slavery had been abolished.

But the war had taken its toll on Abe. The pressures he had faced as president made him look older than he actually was. Rumors of threats against his life were not unusual. Thoughts of death had haunted his dreams. "I long ago made up my mind," he once told a friend, "that if anybody wants to kill me, he will do it."

The atmosphere around the White House

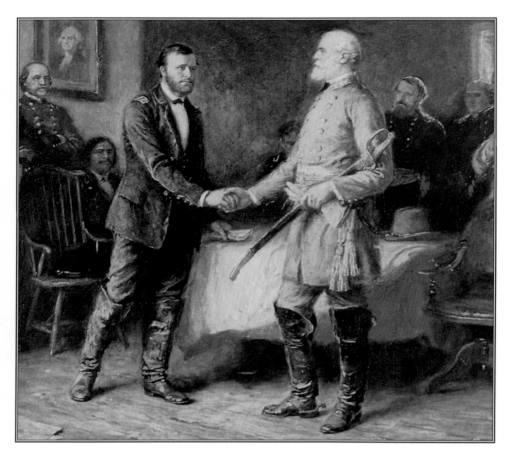

Ulysses S. Grant (left) accepts Robert E. Lee's surrender at Appomattox Court House, Virginia, which marked the end of the Civil War. According to the customs of the time, both men were very polite to each other, even though they had recently faced each other in battle.

became more festive after the war was over. On Good Friday, April 14, 1865, Abe put in a full day's work. That evening, the president and his wife would finally have some time to relax. After dinner, the couple attended a play at Ford's Theater in Washington. The title of the play was *Our American Cousin.* It starred the actress Laura Keene. Abe and his wife were shown to their seats in the presidential box. Major Henry R. Rathbone and his fiancée, Clara Harris, were with them.

At some point during the evening, the president's bodyguard left his post outside the door to the box. He went downstairs to watch the play. At 10:15 P.M., during the third act, a dark figure entered the box. In his hand was a derringer pistol. He reached out toward where the president was sitting. Pointing the gun at the back of Abe's head, he fired. Mrs. Lincoln screamed as the president slumped forward.

Major Rathbone leaped from his seat and lunged at the gunman. The assassin jumped from the box and fell to the stage below. The man was a young actor named John Wilkes Booth, who strongly believed in the Southern cause.

Booth struggled to his feet, having broken a bone in his leg in the fall. He turned to the audience and shouted, "*Sic semper tyrannis!* [Thus always to tyrants!] The South is avenged!" He hobbled off the stage, went out the door, and rode away on a horse he had waiting for him.

Doctors rushed to the president's box, but Abe was already unconscious. "His wound is mortal," said Dr. Charles Leale to another physician. "It is impossible for him to recover." The president was carried out of the theater and brought to a boardinghouse across the street. There he spent the night, with his wife never far from his side.

Government officials arrived at the house throughout the night. Abe's son, Robert, also came to be with his dying father. That same evening, Secretary of State William Seward also had an attempt made on his life. Booth had recruited several others to carry out his plan. They had intended to kill Lincoln, Seward, and Vice President Andrew Johnson.

The Lincoln Memorial in Washington, D.C., is a monument to Abe and his many accomplishments as president. He will always be remembered, not only for freeing slaves, but for reuniting a divided nation.

The next morning, at 7:22 A.M. April 15, 1865, Abraham Lincoln died. He was just 56 years old. A doctor covered the president's body with a sheet. Secretary of War Edwin M. Stanton said, "Now he belongs to the ages."

Abe's body was brought to the White House. Thousands of people passed by his coffin to see the man who had saved the Union. On April 21, his body began the trip by train to its final resting place in Springfield, Illinois. More than seven million people viewed it at the stops made along the way.

Five days later, John Wilkes Booth was shot by federal cavalrymen who trapped him in a barn on a farm in Port Royal, Virginia. Booth refused to surrender. He died as the barn burned to the ground in a fire set by the troops.

While the men were away fighting, wives and sisters also tried to help. In Illinois, women sold home-made items at fairs. The money they received was used to buy supplies for the soldiers. At an 1865 fair, the original draft of the Emancipation Proclamation was auctioned off to raise money. It was then donated to the Chicago Historical Society. Unfortunately, the document was destroyed in the Great Chicago Fire of 1871.

GLOSSARY

abolitionists–those who wanted an immediate end to slavery

aggressor–one who starts a fight

bar–the law profession

campaign–an operation undertaken to achieve some goal

candidates–people running for office

compromise–a settlement of differences in which each side gives up something

frontier–an unexplored area

habeas corpus–guarantees all citizens who are being arrested the right to know the charges that are being made against them

inaugurate–to put into office with an official ceremony

legislature–elected group of people with the power to create laws

plantation–large estate or farm where crops are grown

secede–to withdraw from an organization

slavery–bondage to a master

surveyor–person who determines the boundaries of land

wilderness–wild, unsettled tract of land

CHRONOLOGY

1809   Born on February 12 near Hodgenville, Kentucky.

1834   Elected to first of four terms in Illinois state legislature.

1836   Passes bar exam in Springfield, Illinois.

1842   Marries Mary Todd on November 4.

1846   Elected to U.S. House of Representatives.

1858   Loses Senate bid to Stephen A. Douglas.

1860   Elected 16th president of the United States on November 6.

1861   First shots of Civil War fired at Fort Sumter, South Carolina, on April 12.

1863   Signs Emancipation Proclamation, abolishing slavery, on January 1; Battle of Gettysburg fought in July; delivers Gettysburg Address on November 19.

1865   Begins second term as president on March 4; Robert E. Lee surrenders to Ulysses S. Grant at Appomattox on April 9; shot by John Wilkes Booth at Ford's Theater, Washington, D.C., on April 14; dies on April 15.

CIVIL WAR TIME LINE

1860   Abraham Lincoln is elected president of the United States on November 6. During the next few months, Southern states begin to break away from the Union.

1861   On April 12, the Confederates attack Fort Sumter, South Carolina, and the Civil War begins. Union forces are defeated in Virginia at the First Battle of Bull Run (First Manassas) on July 21 and withdraw to Washington, D.C.

1862   Robert E. Lee is placed in command of the main Confederate army in Virginia in June. Lee defeats the Army of the Potomac at the Second Battle of Bull Run (Second Manassas) in Virginia on August 29–30. On September 17, Union general George B. McClellan turns back Lee's first invasion of the North at Antietam Creek near Sharpsburg, Maryland. It is the bloodiest day of the war.

1863   On January 1, President Lincoln issues the Emancipation Proclamation, freeing slaves in Southern states. Between May 1–6, Lee wins an important victory at Chancellorsville, but key Southern commander Thomas J. "Stonewall" Jackson dies from wounds. In June, Union forces hold the city of Vicksburg, Mississippi, under siege. The people of Vicksburg surrender on July 4. Lee's second invasion of the North during July 1–3 is decisively turned back at Gettysburg, Pennsylvania.

1864   General Grant is made supreme Union commander
        on March 9. Following a series of costly battles, on
        June 19 Grant successfully encircles Lee's troops in
        Petersburg, Virginia. A siege of the town lasts nearly
        a year. Union general William Sherman captures
        Atlanta on September 2 and begins the "March to the
        Sea," a campaign of destruction across Georgia and
        South Carolina. On November 8, Abraham Lincoln
        wins reelection as president.

1865   On April 2, Petersburg, Virginia, falls to the Union.
        Lee attempts to reach Confederate forces in North
        Carolina but is gradually surrounded by Union troops.
        Lee surrenders to Grant on April 9 at Appomattox,
        Virginia, ending the war. Abraham Lincoln is assassinated
        by John Wilkes Booth on April 14.

FURTHER READING

Bracken, Thomas. *Abraham Lincoln.* Philadelphia: Chelsea House Publishers, 1998.

Harness, Cheryl. *Abe Lincoln Goes to Washington, 1837–1865.* Washington, D.C.: National Geographic Society, 1997.

January, Brendan. *The Assassination of Abraham Lincoln.* Danbury, Conn.: Children's Press, 1998.

_____. *The Emancipation Proclamation. Cornerstones of Freedom Series.* Danbury, Conn.: Children's Press, 1998.

_____. *The Lincoln-Douglas Debates.* Danbury, Conn.: Children's Press, 1998.

Judson, Karen. *Abraham Lincoln.* Springfield, N.J.: Enslow Publishers, 1998.

Lincoln, Abraham, et al. *The Gettysburg Address.* Boston: Houghton Mifflin, 1998.

INDEX

PICTURE CREDITS

page

3:   The Library of Congress
6:   National Archives
9:   New Millennium Images
14: The Library of Congress
16: The Library of Congress
19: New Millennium Images
23: The Library of Congress
26: The Library of Congress
28: New Millennium Images
31: The Library of Congress

35: The Library of Congress
38: The Library of Congress
40: The Library of Congress
45: The Library of Congress
49: National Archives
52: The Library of Congress
56: New Millennium Images
63: The Library of Congress
68: The Library of Congress
71: New Millennium Images

ABOUT THE AUTHOR

JOHN F. GRABOWSKI is a computer teacher and free-lance writer, specializing in the fields of sports, education, and comedy. He has degrees in psychology and educational psychology. His body of published work includes 22 books; a nationally syndicated sports column; articles to newspapers, magazines, and the programs of professional sports teams; and comedy material sold to Jay Leno, Joan Rivers, and numerous other comics. He lives in Staten Island, New York, with his wife and daughter.

Senior Consulting Editor **ARTHUR M. SCHLESINGER, JR.** is the leading American historian of our time. He won the Pulitzer Prize for his book *The Age of Jackson* (1945), and again for *A Thousand Days* (1965). This chronicle of the Kennedy Administration also won a National Book Award. He has written many other books, including a multi-volume series, *The Age of Roosevelt.* Professor Schlesinger is the Albert Schweitzer Professor of the Humanities at the City University of New York, and has been involved in several other Chelsea House projects, including the COLONIAL LEADERS series of biographies on the most prominent figures of early American history.